EMMANUEL JOSEPH

The Balanced Equation Productivity + Mindfulness = Stronger Relationships

Copyright © 2025 by Emmanuel Joseph

All rights reserved. No part of this publication may be reproduced, stored or transmitted in any form or by any means, electronic, mechanical, photocopying, recording, scanning, or otherwise without written permission from the publisher. It is illegal to copy this book, post it to a website, or distribute it by any other means without permission.

First edition

*This book was professionally typeset on Reedsy.
Find out more at reedsy.com*

Contents

1 Chapter 1: The Journey Begins — 1
2 Chapter 2: The Science Behind Mindfulness — 3
3 Chapter 3: The Productivity Paradox — 5
4 Chapter 4: Cultivating Mindful Productivity — 7
5 Chapter 5: The Power of Gratitude — 9
6 Chapter 6: Balancing Work and Life — 11
7 Chapter 7: Communication and Connection — 13
8 Chapter 8: The Role of Empathy — 15
9 Chapter 9: The Power of Presence — 16
10 Chapter 10: Building Trust and Intimacy — 17
11 Chapter 11: Navigating Conflict — 19
12 Chapter 12: Fostering Resilience — 21
13 Chapter 13: The Role of Self-Compassion — 23
14 Chapter 14: The Power of Rituals — 25
15 Chapter 15: The Impact of Mindful Leadership — 27
16 Chapter 16: Building a Mindful Community — 29
17 Chapter 17: The Balanced Equation in Action — 31

1

Chapter 1: The Journey Begins

The notion of balancing productivity and mindfulness is often seen as a paradox. For many, the pursuit of productivity seems at odds with the calm introspection associated with mindfulness. However, our journey begins with an understanding that these two concepts are not mutually exclusive. The dance between achieving goals and remaining present in the moment forms the cornerstone of a fulfilling life. We need to strike a balance where both productivity and mindfulness coexist harmoniously.

Productivity is often measured by how much we accomplish in a given timeframe. It is the force that drives us to set goals, prioritize tasks, and achieve milestones. In contrast, mindfulness emphasizes being present and fully engaged with our current activity, allowing us to experience life more vividly. It's about savoring the moment, understanding ourselves, and connecting with the world around us. Combining these two seemingly divergent paths may seem challenging, but it is the key to a well-rounded existence.

When we consciously integrate mindfulness into our productive lives, we create a synergy that can enhance both aspects. Mindfulness helps us focus better on our tasks, reduce stress, and improve our overall well-being. Meanwhile, productivity gives structure to our mindfulness practices, ensuring we don't lose sight of our goals. The first step in this journey is recognizing the value each brings to our lives and finding ways to meld them together.

As we embark on this journey, it's important to remember that balance doesn't mean equal parts of each. Rather, it means allowing each to complement the other in a way that supports our overall well-being. By embracing both productivity and mindfulness, we lay the foundation for stronger relationships, as we become more present and engaged with those around us. This holistic approach fosters deeper connections and a greater sense of fulfillment in our personal and professional lives.

2

Chapter 2: The Science Behind Mindfulness

Mindfulness has gained significant attention in recent years, and for good reason. Scientific research has demonstrated the numerous benefits of mindfulness practices, from reducing stress and anxiety to improving cognitive function and emotional regulation. By understanding the science behind mindfulness, we can better appreciate its role in enhancing our productivity and relationships.

At its core, mindfulness involves paying attention to our thoughts, feelings, and sensations without judgment. This heightened awareness allows us to observe our inner experiences and gain insights into our behavior patterns. Neuroscientific studies have shown that mindfulness practices can lead to structural and functional changes in the brain, particularly in areas associated with attention, self-regulation, and empathy. These changes help us become more focused, resilient, and compassionate.

One of the key mechanisms through which mindfulness affects the brain is neuroplasticity, the brain's ability to reorganize itself by forming new neural connections. Regular mindfulness practice has been shown to increase the density of gray matter in regions responsible for learning, memory, and emotional regulation. Additionally, mindfulness can reduce the activity of the amygdala, the brain's fear center, leading to decreased stress and anxiety levels.

As we integrate mindfulness into our daily lives, we not only improve our mental and emotional well-being but also enhance our productivity. By being fully present and engaged in our tasks, we can work more efficiently and effectively. Moreover, mindfulness helps us develop better interpersonal skills, as we become more attuned to the needs and emotions of others. This heightened awareness fosters stronger relationships, as we are better equipped to navigate social interactions with empathy and understanding.

3

Chapter 3: The Productivity Paradox

The pursuit of productivity is often associated with the hustle culture, where individuals are encouraged to work tirelessly and achieve more in less time. However, this relentless drive for productivity can lead to burnout, stress, and strained relationships. The productivity paradox arises when our efforts to be more productive ultimately hinder our overall well-being and effectiveness.

One of the main reasons behind the productivity paradox is the misconception that being busy equates to being productive. In reality, true productivity involves working smarter, not harder. It requires us to prioritize our tasks, manage our time effectively, and maintain a healthy work-life balance. By incorporating mindfulness into our productivity practices, we can create a more sustainable and fulfilling approach to achieving our goals.

Mindfulness helps us break free from the cycle of constant busyness by encouraging us to slow down and focus on the present moment. This practice allows us to better understand our priorities, make more informed decisions, and allocate our time and energy more effectively. By being mindful of our actions and choices, we can avoid the trap of multitasking and instead concentrate on one task at a time, leading to higher quality work and greater satisfaction.

Moreover, mindfulness can help us develop a growth mindset, where we view challenges and setbacks as opportunities for learning and growth. This perspective enables us to approach our work with curiosity and resilience, rather than fear and anxiety. As a result, we become more adaptable and better equipped to handle the demands of our personal and professional lives. By embracing mindfulness, we can transcend the productivity paradox and create a more balanced and fulfilling life.

4

Chapter 4: Cultivating Mindful Productivity

Mindful productivity is the practice of combining productivity strategies with mindfulness techniques to achieve a balanced and effective approach to our tasks and goals. By cultivating mindful productivity, we can enhance our focus, reduce stress, and foster stronger relationships. This chapter explores practical ways to integrate mindfulness into our productivity practices.

One of the most effective ways to cultivate mindful productivity is through the practice of mindfulness meditation. This technique involves setting aside time each day to sit quietly and focus on our breath, allowing our thoughts to come and go without judgment. Regular meditation practice can help us develop greater self-awareness, emotional regulation, and mental clarity, which in turn improves our ability to manage our time and tasks effectively.

Another key aspect of mindful productivity is the practice of mindful breaks. Rather than working tirelessly for hours on end, it is essential to take regular breaks to recharge and refocus. During these breaks, we can engage in mindfulness activities such as deep breathing exercises, stretching, or taking a walk in nature. These practices help us clear our minds, reduce stress, and return to our tasks with renewed energy and focus.

Additionally, incorporating mindfulness into our daily routines can enhance our overall well-being and productivity. Simple practices such as mindful eating, where we pay attention to the taste, texture, and aroma of our food, or mindful listening, where we fully engage in conversations without distractions, can help us develop greater presence and awareness in our lives. By being more mindful in our everyday activities, we can create a more balanced and fulfilling approach to productivity.

5

Chapter 5: The Power of Gratitude

Gratitude is a powerful emotion that can significantly impact our well-being, productivity, and relationships. By cultivating an attitude of gratitude, we can foster a more positive mindset, enhance our emotional resilience, and strengthen our connections with others. This chapter explores the science behind gratitude and practical ways to incorporate it into our daily lives.

Research has shown that practicing gratitude can lead to numerous physical, psychological, and social benefits. Physically, gratitude has been linked to better sleep, reduced inflammation, and improved heart health. Psychologically, it can increase our overall happiness, reduce stress and anxiety, and promote a greater sense of life satisfaction. Socially, gratitude helps us build stronger relationships by fostering empathy, compassion, and mutual appreciation.

One of the most effective ways to cultivate gratitude is through the practice of gratitude journaling. This involves regularly writing down the things we are grateful for, whether they are big or small. By reflecting on the positive aspects of our lives, we can shift our focus away from negativity and develop a more optimistic outlook. Gratitude journaling also helps us become more aware of the support and kindness we receive from others, which in turn strengthens our relationships.

In addition to journaling, we can practice gratitude in our daily interactions by expressing appreciation and recognition to those around us. Simple acts of kindness, such as thanking a colleague for their help or acknowledging a friend's support, can go a long way in fostering a culture of gratitude. By cultivating an attitude of gratitude, we can enhance our well-being, boost our productivity, and build stronger, more meaningful relationships.

6

Chapter 6: Balancing Work and Life

Achieving a healthy work-life balance is essential for our overall well-being and the strength of our relationships. When work demands become overwhelming, it can lead to burnout, stress, and strained connections with our loved ones. This chapter explores strategies for balancing work and life, and how mindfulness can play a crucial role in achieving this balance.

One of the key principles of work-life balance is setting boundaries between our professional and personal lives. This involves establishing clear limits on our working hours, creating dedicated time for family and self-care, and ensuring that work-related tasks do not encroach on our personal time. By setting boundaries, we can create a more sustainable and fulfilling approach to both our work and personal lives.

Mindfulness can help us maintain this balance by encouraging us to be fully present in each aspect of our lives. When we are at work, mindfulness allows us to focus on our tasks with clarity and intention, leading to greater productivity and job satisfaction. Conversely, when we are with our loved ones, mindfulness helps us engage more deeply in our interactions, fostering stronger connections and a greater sense of fulfillment.

Another important aspect of work-life balance is prioritizing self-care. This involves taking time to nurture our physical, mental, and emotional well-being through activities such as exercise, meditation, hobbies, and relaxation.

By prioritizing self-care, we can recharge our energy, reduce stress, and enhance our overall well-being. Mindfulness practices can support our self-care efforts by helping us become more attuned to our needs and better equipped to manage stress.

Incorporating mindfulness into our work-life balance also involves cultivating a sense of gratitude and appreciation for both our professional and personal lives. By recognizing the value of our work and the importance of our relationships, we can create a more harmonious and fulfilling approach to life. This balance not only enhances our overall well-being but also strengthens our connections with others, as we become more present and engaged in our interactions.

7

Chapter 7: Communication and Connection

Effective communication is the foundation of strong relationships. It allows us to express our thoughts and feelings, understand others, and resolve conflicts. Mindfulness can play a significant role in improving our communication skills by helping us become more present, attentive, and empathetic in our interactions.

One of the key aspects of mindful communication is active listening. This involves fully engaging with the speaker, paying attention to their words, tone, and body language, and providing feedback that shows we understand and value their perspective. By practicing active listening, we can create a more supportive and understanding environment, which fosters deeper connections and trust.

Another important aspect of mindful communication is being aware of our own emotions and reactions. Mindfulness helps us recognize when we are feeling stressed, frustrated, or defensive, and allows us to respond more thoughtfully rather than reacting impulsively. This self-awareness enables us to communicate more effectively and navigate difficult conversations with greater ease and compassion.

In addition to active listening and emotional awareness, mindful communication also involves expressing ourselves clearly and respectfully. By choosing our words carefully and being mindful of our tone and body language, we can convey our thoughts and feelings in a way that is more likely to be understood and appreciated by others. This approach not only enhances our relationships but also helps us build a more positive and supportive social network.

8

Chapter 8: The Role of Empathy

Empathy is the ability to understand and share the feelings of others. It is a crucial component of strong relationships, as it allows us to connect with others on a deeper level and provide support and compassion. Mindfulness can help us develop greater empathy by increasing our awareness of our own emotions and the emotions of those around us.

One of the ways mindfulness enhances empathy is by helping us become more attuned to the present moment. When we are fully present, we are better able to notice and understand the subtle cues that indicate how others are feeling. This heightened awareness allows us to respond more empathetically and provide the support and understanding that others need.

Mindfulness also helps us develop greater self-awareness, which is essential for empathy. By understanding our own emotions and reactions, we can better recognize and relate to the emotions of others. This self-awareness enables us to approach our interactions with greater compassion and understanding, which fosters stronger connections and trust.

Practicing mindfulness can also help us develop a more open and non-judgmental attitude towards others. By observing our thoughts and feelings without judgment, we can cultivate a greater sense of acceptance and understanding for the experiences and perspectives of others. This openness allows us to connect more deeply with others and build stronger, more supportive relationships.

9

Chapter 9: The Power of Presence

Being present in our interactions with others is essential for building strong relationships. When we are fully engaged and attentive, we create a sense of connection and understanding that fosters trust and intimacy. Mindfulness can help us cultivate this presence by encouraging us to focus on the present moment and let go of distractions.

One of the key benefits of being present is that it allows us to fully experience and appreciate our interactions with others. When we are mindful, we can truly listen to what others are saying, observe their body language, and respond with empathy and understanding. This level of engagement creates a deeper sense of connection and strengthens our relationships.

Being present also helps us manage our own emotions and reactions more effectively. By staying focused on the present moment, we can avoid getting caught up in negative thoughts or worries about the past or future. This emotional regulation allows us to respond more thoughtfully and compassionately in our interactions, which fosters a more supportive and understanding environment.

In addition to enhancing our relationships, being present can also improve our overall well-being. When we are fully engaged in our activities and interactions, we can experience greater satisfaction and fulfillment in our lives. By cultivating mindfulness and presence, we can create a more balanced and meaningful approach to our personal and professional lives.

10

Chapter 10: Building Trust and Intimacy

Trust and intimacy are the foundations of strong relationships. They allow us to feel safe, supported, and understood, and enable us to share our thoughts, feelings, and experiences with others. Mindfulness can play a significant role in building trust and intimacy by helping us become more present, empathetic, and authentic in our interactions.

One of the ways mindfulness helps build trust is by encouraging us to be more present and attentive in our interactions. When we are fully engaged and focused on the other person, we create a sense of connection and understanding that fosters trust. This presence also allows us to better understand and respond to the needs and emotions of others, which strengthens our relationships.

Mindfulness also helps us develop greater self-awareness and emotional regulation, which are essential for building trust and intimacy. By understanding our own emotions and reactions, we can communicate more effectively and navigate conflicts with greater ease and compassion. This self-awareness also allows us to be more authentic and genuine in our interactions, which fosters deeper connections and trust.

In addition to presence and self-awareness, mindfulness helps us cultivate a sense of empathy and compassion for others. By observing our thoughts and feelings without judgment, we can develop a greater sense of acceptance and understanding for the experiences and perspectives of others. This empathy allows us to connect more deeply with others and build stronger, more supportive relationships.

11

Chapter 11: Navigating Conflict

Conflict is an inevitable part of any relationship, and how we navigate it can significantly impact the strength and stability of our connections. Mindfulness can help us approach conflicts with greater awareness, empathy, and understanding, allowing us to resolve issues more effectively and maintain healthy relationships.

One of the key benefits of mindfulness in conflict resolution is that it helps us become more aware of our own emotions and reactions. By observing our thoughts and feelings without judgment, we can recognize when we are feeling stressed, angry, or defensive, and respond more thoughtfully rather than reacting impulsively. This self-awareness allows us to approach conflicts with greater calm and clarity, which facilitates more productive and constructive discussions.

Mindfulness also helps us develop greater empathy and understanding for the perspectives and emotions of others. By being fully present and attentive in our interactions, we can better understand the underlying needs and concerns that drive conflicts. This empathy allows us to approach conflicts with greater compassion and a willingness to find mutually beneficial solutions.

In addition to self-awareness and empathy, mindfulness helps us cultivate a sense of acceptance and non-judgment. By observing our thoughts and feelings without judgment, we can develop a greater sense of openness and understanding for the experiences and perspectives of others. This acceptance allows us to approach conflicts with a more collaborative and solution-focused mindset, which fosters stronger relationships and greater trust.

12

Chapter 12: Fostering Resilience

Resilience is the ability to bounce back from setbacks and challenges, and it is a crucial component of strong relationships. Mindfulness can help us develop greater resilience by enhancing our self-awareness, emotional regulation, and ability to cope with stress and adversity.

One of the key ways mindfulness fosters resilience is by helping us become more aware of our thoughts and emotions. By observing our inner experiences without judgment, we can develop greater insight into our behavior patterns and responses to stress. This self-awareness allows us to identify and address the underlying causes of our stress and develop more effective coping strategies.

Mindfulness also helps us develop greater emotional regulation, which is essential for resilience. By practicing mindfulness techniques such as meditation and deep breathing, we can calm our minds and bodies and reduce the impact of stress on our well-being. This emotional regulation enables us to approach challenges with greater calm and clarity, which enhances our ability to cope with adversity.

In addition to self-awareness and emotional regulation, mindfulness helps us cultivate a sense of acceptance and non-judgment towards ourselves and our experiences. By observing our thoughts and feelings without judgment, we can develop greater self-compassion and a more positive mindset. This acceptance allows us to approach challenges with greater resilience and adaptability, which fosters stronger relationships and greater well-being.

13

Chapter 13: The Role of Self-Compassion

Self-compassion is the practice of treating ourselves with kindness and understanding, especially during times of difficulty and failure. It is a crucial component of well-being and strong relationships, as it helps us develop greater emotional resilience and a more positive mindset. Mindfulness can play a significant role in cultivating self-compassion by encouraging us to observe our thoughts and feelings without judgment.

One of the key benefits of self-compassion is that it helps us develop greater emotional resilience. By treating ourselves with kindness and understanding, we can better cope with setbacks and challenges and maintain a more positive outlook. Mindfulness helps us cultivate self-compassion by encouraging us to observe our thoughts and feelings without judgment, which fosters a greater sense of acceptance and understanding towards ourselves.

Self-compassion also helps us develop a more positive mindset and a greater sense of self-worth. By treating ourselves with kindness and understanding, we can counteract negative self-talk and build a more positive and supportive inner dialogue. This positive mindset enhances our overall well-being and helps us approach our relationships with greater empathy and compassion.

In addition to emotional resilience and a positive mindset, self-compassion helps us develop stronger relationships by fostering greater empathy and understanding towards others. By treating ourselves with kindness and understanding, we can better appreciate the experiences and perspectives of others and approach our interactions with greater compassion and support. This empathy and understanding strengthen our connections and build a more supportive and positive social network.

14

Chapter 14: The Power of Rituals

Rituals are the routines and practices that give structure and meaning to our lives. They can help us create a sense of stability and predictability, which enhances our overall well-being and strengthens our relationships. Mindfulness can play a significant role in creating meaningful rituals that enhance our overall well-being and strengthen our relationships. This chapter explores the power of rituals and how we can incorporate mindfulness into our daily routines to create a more balanced and fulfilling life.

One of the key benefits of rituals is that they provide a sense of stability and predictability in our lives. By establishing regular routines and practices, we can create a sense of structure and order that helps us navigate the complexities of our personal and professional lives. Mindfulness can enhance these rituals by encouraging us to be fully present and engaged in our activities, which fosters a greater sense of appreciation and fulfillment.

Rituals also help us create meaningful connections with others by providing opportunities for shared experiences and interactions. Whether it's a family dinner, a weekly catch-up with friends, or a team-building activity at work, these rituals create a sense of belonging and camaraderie that strengthens our relationships. Mindfulness can enhance these connections by helping us become more attuned to the needs and emotions of others, which fosters greater empathy and understanding.

Incorporating mindfulness into our rituals can also help us develop greater self-awareness and emotional regulation. By observing our thoughts and feelings without judgment, we can better understand our behavior patterns and responses to stress. This self-awareness allows us to create rituals that support our well-being and help us manage stress more effectively. By cultivating mindfulness in our daily routines, we can create a more balanced and fulfilling approach to life.

15

Chapter 15: The Impact of Mindful Leadership

Mindful leadership is the practice of leading with awareness, empathy, and compassion. It is a crucial component of strong relationships and effective teamwork, as it helps create a supportive and inclusive environment where individuals can thrive. This chapter explores the principles of mindful leadership and how we can cultivate these qualities in our personal and professional lives.

One of the key principles of mindful leadership is self-awareness. By understanding our own emotions, strengths, and limitations, we can lead with greater authenticity and integrity. Mindfulness helps us develop this self-awareness by encouraging us to observe our thoughts and feelings without judgment, which fosters a greater sense of acceptance and understanding towards ourselves.

Mindful leadership also involves empathy and compassion towards others. By being fully present and attentive in our interactions, we can better understand the needs and emotions of our team members and provide the support and guidance they need to succeed. This empathy and compassion create a more inclusive and supportive environment, which fosters greater collaboration and trust.

In addition to self-awareness and empathy, mindful leadership involves the practice of active listening and effective communication. By fully engaging with our team members and providing clear and constructive feedback, we can create a more open and transparent environment where individuals feel valued and understood. Mindfulness helps us develop these communication skills by encouraging us to be present and attentive in our interactions, which fosters greater understanding and connection.

16

Chapter 16: Building a Mindful Community

Building a mindful community involves creating a supportive and inclusive environment where individuals can thrive and grow. It requires a commitment to mindfulness practices and a willingness to support and uplift others. This chapter explores the principles of building a mindful community and how we can cultivate these qualities in our personal and professional lives.

One of the key principles of building a mindful community is the practice of empathy and compassion. By being fully present and attentive in our interactions, we can better understand the needs and emotions of others and provide the support and guidance they need to succeed. This empathy and compassion create a more inclusive and supportive environment, which fosters greater collaboration and trust.

Building a mindful community also involves the practice of active listening and effective communication. By fully engaging with others and providing clear and constructive feedback, we can create a more open and transparent environment where individuals feel valued and understood. Mindfulness helps us develop these communication skills by encouraging us to be present and attentive in our interactions, which fosters greater understanding and connection.

In addition to empathy and effective communication, building a mindful community involves a commitment to self-care and well-being. By prioritizing our own well-being and supporting the well-being of others, we can create a more balanced and fulfilling environment where individuals can thrive. Mindfulness practices such as meditation, gratitude journaling, and mindful breaks can help us develop this commitment to self-care and well-being, which enhances our overall quality of life.

17

Chapter 17: The Balanced Equation in Action

The journey of balancing productivity and mindfulness is an ongoing process that requires commitment, self-awareness, and a willingness to grow and adapt. By integrating these principles into our daily lives, we can create a more balanced and fulfilling approach to our personal and professional lives. This chapter explores practical ways to put the balanced equation of productivity and mindfulness into action.

One of the key steps in putting the balanced equation into action is setting clear goals and priorities. By identifying what is most important to us and creating a plan to achieve our goals, we can maintain a sense of direction and focus in our lives. Mindfulness helps us stay present and engaged in our tasks, which enhances our ability to achieve our goals and maintain a sense of balance.

Another important step in putting the balanced equation into action is creating a supportive and inclusive environment. By fostering empathy, compassion, and effective communication in our interactions, we can build stronger relationships and create a more positive and collaborative environment. Mindfulness helps us develop these qualities by encouraging us to be fully present and attentive in our interactions, which fosters greater understanding and connection.

In addition to setting goals and creating a supportive environment, putting the balanced equation into action involves a commitment to self-care and well-being. By prioritizing our own well-being and supporting the well-being of others, we can create a more balanced and fulfilling approach to life. Mindfulness practices such as meditation, gratitude journaling, and mindful breaks can help us develop this commitment to self-care and well-being, which enhances our overall quality of life.

By embracing the balanced equation of productivity and mindfulness, we can create a more harmonious and fulfilling approach to our personal and professional lives. This holistic approach not only enhances our well-being but also strengthens our relationships and helps us achieve our goals with greater clarity and intention. The journey may be challenging, but the rewards are well worth the effort.

Description:

In a world that constantly demands more from us, striking a balance between productivity and mindfulness can seem like an impossible task. **"The Balanced Equation"** delves into the intricate relationship between these two essential facets of our lives and reveals how their harmonious integration can lead to stronger, more meaningful relationships.

Through 17 insightful chapters, this book explores the science behind mindfulness, the paradox of productivity, and practical strategies to cultivate mindful productivity. It highlights the importance of gratitude, effective communication, empathy, and presence in building trust and intimacy within our relationships. Furthermore, it emphasizes the role of self-compassion, resilience, and mindful leadership in creating a supportive and inclusive community.

"The Balanced Equation" offers readers a holistic approach to balancing their personal and professional lives. By integrating mindfulness into our daily routines and prioritizing self-care and well-being, we can achieve our goals with greater clarity and intention while fostering deeper connections with those around us.

Whether you are a professional seeking to enhance your productivity, a leader aiming to create a more empathetic and inclusive environment,

CHAPTER 17: THE BALANCED EQUATION IN ACTION

or an individual looking to strengthen your relationships, **"The Balanced Equation"** provides valuable insights and practical tools to help you thrive in all aspects of your life. Embark on this transformative journey and discover the power of balancing productivity and mindfulness to create a more fulfilling and harmonious existence.

www.ingramcontent.com/pod-product-compliance
Lightning Source LLC
LaVergne TN
LVHW020501080526
838202LV00057B/6082